D1228701

ART PROFILES
For Kids
RAPHAEL

Mitchell Lane
PUBLISHERS

P.O. Box 196
Hockessin, Delaware 19707
Visit us on the web: www.mitchelllane.com
Comments? email us: mitchelllane@mitchelllane.com

ART PROFILES FOR KIDS

Titles in the Series

Art Profiles
For Kids

RAPHAEL

Juliet Mofford

Mitchell Lane
PUBLISHERS

P.O. Box 196
Hockessin, Delaware 19707
Visit us on the web: www.mitchelllane.com
Comments? email us: mitchelllane@mitchelllane.com

Mitchell Lane
PUBLISHERS

Printing   1   2   3   4   5   6   7   8   9

Library of Congress Cataloging-in-Publication Data
Mofford, Juliet Haines.
Raphael / by Juliet Haines Mofford.
p. cm. — (Art profiles for kids)
Includes bibliographical references and index.
ISBN 978-1-58415-745-8 (library bound)
1. Raphael, 1483–1520—Juvenile literature. 2. Painters—Italy—Biography—Juvenile literature.
I. Raphael, 1483–1520. II. Title.
ND623.R2M73 2009
759.5—dc22
[B]
                                                                          2009001323

ABOUT THE AUTHOR: After challenging careers as a teacher, librarian, and museum educator, Juliet Haines Mofford became a full-time writer and historical researcher. Her articles and stories have appeared in more than one hundred magazines and newspapers. Curricula, videos, and plays she scripted are currently in use in classrooms and museums. *Raphael,* her ninth book, is her first for Mitchell Lane Publishers.

Juliet has lived in eleven states and six foreign countries, and has taught in Japan, Spain, and the West Indies. She has a degree from Tufts University, with graduate studies in art history at Boston University and Goethe-Universität in Germany. She has seen most of the works discussed in this book.

She and her husband have three grown children and four granddaughters and live on the Maine coast.

ABOUT THE COVER: The images on the cover are paintings by the various artists in this series.

PUBLISHER'S NOTE: The facts on which this story is based have been thoroughly researched. Documentation of such research appears on page 46. While every possible effort has been made to ensure accuracy, the publisher will not assume liability for damages caused by inaccuracies in the data, and makes no warranty on the accuracy of the information contained herein.

To reflect current usage, we have chosen to use the secular era designations BCE ("before the common era") and CE ("of the common era") instead of the traditional designations BC ("before Christ") and AD (*anno Domini,* "in the year of the Lord").

Art Profiles for Kids

Saint George and the Dragon. The Duke of Urbino commissioned Raphael to paint several versions of this scene for the King of England. Art historians have praised Raphael's ability to express dramatic themes, but think the artist was less skillful at painting animals.

CHAPTER 1

one

The Court Painter's Son

"Have all the banners been hung? Are the musicians in place?" Giovanni Santi called. "Duke Guidobaldo and his party will be arriving any moment! Raffaello, did you put away the paint buckets?"

"Yes, Papa," the nine-year-old boy replied. He loved the excitement that always surrounded the duke's return to court. Since Raffaello's mother's death the year before, he had spent most of his time at his father's side in the ducal palace. Giovanni, known as Sanzio, served the Montefeltro family as painter and poet in the Court of Urbino, located in the mountains east of Florence. He also wrote and produced pageants, musical shows, and plays for the duke's large court and many guests. The youngest student in his father's workshop, Raphael already knew how to grind pigments from flowers and berries to make paints, and the correct way to trim and mount brushes.

Even though Raphael was the master's son, he was expected to run errands and sweep the studio floor. He had become increasingly familiar with the different materials artists used, and his drawing ability was improving every day. Along with his other students, Giovanni taught Raphael how to prepare walls to receive frescoes and allowed his son to help build the scaffolding to reach ceiling decorations. Young as he was, Raphael designed banners for pageants and painted scenery for Papa's plays.

Raphael spent his childhood surrounded by art and culture. Oil and tempera works by Flemish artists hung on the palace walls. Painters from Spain were invited to court. Italian masters like Masaccio (1401–1428), called

the "father of Renaissance art" by some, decorated the ducal palace in his day. Although Paolo Uccello, another court painter, died in 1475, the influence of his solid forms and use of perspective left its legacy on the Urbino style. Piero della Francesca (1416–1492), who, like the architect Donato Bramante, applied laws of mathematics to perspective in art, was hired to paint there. Raphael practiced draftsmanship by copying great works around the ducal palace. Like Giovanni's other students, Raphael studied the human body by molding clay sculptures. Sketching with sanguine (pencils made from red clay), the boy drew hands in different poses, struggled to make limbs look real beneath drapery, and practiced facial expressions.

Poets, philosophers, painters, sculptors, architects, and musicians were all highly respected at the elegant Court of Urbino. Wooden mosaics of various colors and textures covered interior walls. Landscaped courtyards and hanging gardens lay outside the palace windows. Works by classical authors were read aloud at mealtimes, along with poems by Giovanni Santi. Raphael's father wrote twenty-three books of poetry celebrating the duke's family.[1] Artists, writers, and intellectuals came here from all over Italy as well as other countries, and young Raphael tried to meet them all. He listened, observed, and learned.

Giorgio Vasari, who wrote about the lives of Italian Renaissance artists, said that Raphael's father, recognizing his son's talent, took him to Perugia, the Umbrian capital, when he was about eight. He was to become an apprentice in the studio of Pietro Vanucci, known as Perugino.

"My boy, Raffaello, has a special gift," one can imagine Giovanni saying with a father's pride. "I have taught him all I can. The time has come for my son to study under the most successful painter in all Italy." It was the dream of every boy who wished to become an artist: to be accepted in the workshop of a great master. One needed only to choose the artist whose style he most admired, and one with good connections, to assure his future.

Some scholars believe Raphael was eighteen when he became Perugino's assistant, while art historian Bette Talvacchia claims it is "unclear whether or not Raphael was ever a part of Perugino's workshop as either

student or assistant."[2] Whatever the truth, Perugino's style definitely had great influence on Raphael's early work. By 1500, the young painter was receiving commissions of his own in Perugia.

Perugino was famous for achieving harmony and balance in his paintings, as well as the way he organized human figures within space. His dramatic religious scenes are usually staged in front of architectural backgrounds. From Perugino, Raphael also learned much about the use of perspective and color.

Giovanni Santi died in 1494, and Raphael probably continued living with his stepmother. His father's brother, Bartolomeo, was appointed guardian, though he argued with Santi's widow over the family estate. Raphael was only eleven when he inherited his father's studio, and by the time he turned sixteen, he was called "master."

The earliest documented work by Raphael, painted when he was seventeen with another student of his father's, was a San Nicola of Tolentino altarpiece in Città di Castello, near Urbino. Due to earthquake damage, only fragments remain.

He painted *Vision of a Knight: An Allegory* in 1504. Adapted from an epic poem about the Second Punic War, Scipio, a young soldier, sees two women in a dream: one is Virtue; the other, Pleasure. Virtue, offering a sword in one hand and a book in the other, promises the knight scholarship, along with glory in battle. Pleasure, with flowing locks and beautiful clothing, symbolizes love. She offers Scipio a flower and promises him the easy life, symbolized by the sunlit lake and tranquil mountains behind. The painting is as carefully balanced as a scale with the tree in the middle. According to art historian Hugo Chapman, this is one of only two non religious works, besides portraits, that Raphael painted before moving to Rome.[3]

Between 1504 and 1506, Raphael painted two versions of *St. George and the Dragon* at the request of the Montefeltro Court. Both depict the hero vanquishing his enemy, which symbolizes the power of good over evil. Henry VII, King of England, bestowed the Order of the Garter upon Duke Federico da Montefeltro. After Federico's death, his son, Duke

Vision of a Knight: An Allegory. Raphael enjoyed creating narrative paintings. Using symbols, he retells a story from classical Roman poetry. The young artist already understands how to express harmony and grace, and his love of nature is also evident.

Guidobaldo, was awarded the same honor. Raphael's painting was likely meant as a gift for the British monarch, since St. George is the patron saint of England.[4] The artist signed his name on the horse's harness.

Raphael's *Marriage of the Virgin,* painted for the Church of San Francesco in Città di Castello (1504), marks the end of Raphael's Perugino phase, according to scholars. Figures in the foreground illustrate a religious story before a piazza, and smaller figures lead the viewer's eye toward the temple in the background. Raphael placed his figures in three groups, so viewers' eyes move from one to another. Along with architecture, Perugino passed on his interest in Umbrian and Tuscan landscapes to his protégé. Raphael added a note of humor to this holy scene. The males on the right represent suitors Mary rejected when she picked Joseph. One disappointed young man angrily breaks a stick across his leg. So that this painting would never be mistaken for Perugino, the artist wrote *Raffelo da Urbino* across the temple.

Raphael was greatly admired during his lifetime and long after. Giorgio Vasari praised him highly, writing: "Heaven sometimes showers upon one single person, all the favors and precious gifts that are usually shared among a great many people. This was clearly the case with Raphael Sanzio, an artist as talented as he was gracious, endowed by nature with the goodness and modesty to be found among those exceptional men whose gentle humanity is enhanced by a pleasing manner, expressing itself in courteous behavior at all times and towards all persons. . . . By nature, Raphael was so full of kindness and brimming with charity that the very animals honored him. In his presence even the most ambitious artists worked together in concord."[5]

At twenty, Raphael thought the time had come to pursue the next step in his career. He would move to Florence, where art was flourishing under Medici rule. The city, the wealthiest in Italy, was Europe's leading center of art. In his pocket, Raphael carried a letter of introduction from a member of the Montefeltro family and the pope's sister-in-law. Dated October 1, 1504, and addressed to a government official of Florence, it begins, "The bearer of this will be found to be Raffaele, painter of Urbino, who being greatly gifted in his profession, has determined to spend some time in Florence to

Marriage of the Virgin. Considered Raphael's first major work, this altarpiece shows Pietro Perugino's strong influence. The action takes place in the foreground as if the main characters are performing on stage, while other figures are grouped to direct the eye across the piazza to the impressive temple in back. Raphael has outdone his teacher.

study. And because his father was most worthy and I was very attached to him, and the son is a sensible and well mannered young man . . ."[6]

Thus, the young artist left his Umbrian home to resettle in Florence. Raphael was eager to observe the works of great artists, past and present. In these new surroundings, his themes and artistic style would change, and his remarkable talent would blossom.

The Dukes of Urbino

Urbino was a walled town and a Papal State. Tiers of houses climbed up the rocky hill, topped by a palace with 250 rooms. Federico da Montefeltro became Duke of Urbino in 1444 and governed forty years. Since Urbino lacked soil sufficient for farming and was not near major trade routes, the duke filled the treasury by serving as a condottiere (captain of mercenary soldiers). Although wars among ruling nobles and city-states often kept him away, Federico maintained peace and prosperity at home.

Raphael's,
Guidobaldo da Montefeltro

During the Renaissance, Italian cities competed to build the finest architectural monuments and own the most beautiful works of art. Artists created projects to glorify princes and popes. Duke Federico renovated and enlarged his palace, and was determined to make Urbino the ideal city. A contemporary remarked, "The country he ruled was a wondrous sight."[7]

Federico died seven months before Raphael's birth, and was succeeded by his son, Guidobaldo Montefeltro. In 1502, Cesare Borgia, son of Pope Alexander VI, attacked the peaceful duchy of Urbino, sending the duke and duchess into exile. Not until Pope Alexander died in August 1503 could the Montefeltro family safely return. The new pope, Julius II, was related to the duke and appointed him captain general of the church.

Under Duke Guidobaldo and his brilliant wife, Elisabetta Gonzaga, Urbino flourished once more. No expense was spared in making it first in art and culture. When Raphael was a boy there, five hundred people served the court. Great works of art, tapestries, and decorative walls of inlaid wood adorned the palace. Thirty scribes kept busy copying books by hand in the duke's library.[8] One of Europe's largest, the library held more than a thousand works on a variety of subjects, including science, the art of war, and astrology. Poets read aloud, minstrels played their lutes and sang, and costumed actors regularly performed plays.[9]

Raphael's *Elisabetta Gonzaga*

Madonna of the Chair (Madonna della Seggiola or *Madonna della Sedia).*
Raphael won lasting fame for his graceful lifelike renderings of mother and
child. Both look out of the tondo, inviting us to join this tender family scene.
The figures crowd the space, pushing Mary's legs upward, yet the vertical
chair gives balance to the whole. Raphael paid careful attention to detail in
textures of the clothing.

two

Florence: "School of the World"

The Renaissance was marked by change and new possibilities. From *rinascita*, meaning "rebirth," this cultural revolution began in Italy around 1300 CE and moved north through Europe, lasting until the 1600s. World exploration, new scientific discoveries, and an appreciation of the classical past marked the period. Increased trade led to the growth of cities and exposure to diverse cultures. Banks developed, along with a new merchant class with money to spend on art and architecture. Humanism, the idea that mankind was the center of everything and in charge of its own destiny, became the guiding philosophy. People valued their ability to reason and gained new confidence through self-expression. Johann Gutenberg's invention of a printing press with movable type made books widely available, so people were able to rediscover the literature, art, architecture, and philosophy of ancient Greece and Rome.

The ideal "Renaissance man" was someone who was successful in several fields of endeavor or an artist who created beautiful works using different mediums. Leonardo da Vinci, Michelangelo, and Raphael were such men, and are still considered the three greatest artists of the High Renaissance.

Renaissance artists showed new appreciation for the natural world. The landscapes they painted reflected sunlight shimmering through trees and colors of changing seasons upon distant hills. By using live models, studying classical statues, and even dissecting corpses, Renaissance artists learned how to make the human body more realistic.

15

CHAPTER 2

It was one of the best times in history to be an artist. The independent city-states of Italy, known individually as the Republic of Florence, Kingdom of Naples, Duchy of Milan, and the Papal States, competed with one another to attract the most talented painters, sculptors, and architects to glorify their rulers and beautify their towns. Merchants and princes could afford to hire artists and architects to build private villas and family chapels and to paint their portraits. The Catholic Church offered generous commissions to favored artists.

When Raphael arrived in Florence in 1504, the city was filled with artists. Vasari called it "the school of the world." Prosperous patrons were continually seeking artists with new styles, techniques, and themes. Raphael was confident he could get commissions based on the work he'd already done in the Perugino style—especially since Perugino ran a workshop in the city.

The talk of the town was the giant statue of *David* in Piazza della Signoria, which had taken Michelangelo Buonarroti four years to carve. Influenced by statues of classical gods and heroes, *David* celebrated the beauty and balance of the human body poised for action. When Michelangelo's work was unveiled in 1504, it was considered the finest sculpture since Roman times.

Raphael also stood spellbound before da Vinci's *Adoration of the Magi,* though the painting was unfinished. "So this is sfumato," Raphael may have been thinking as he studied the way the artist blended light and shadow. "Now I understand why da Vinci is considered the greatest artist alive. The genius is thirty years older than I am," Raphael likely reminded himself. "Perhaps, when I am his age, I will be able to paint with the same balance of composition and control of light and shadow."

During his next four years in Florence, Raphael absorbed the work of great artists, living and dead. He made friends with other painters and was introduced to patrons. Vasari says that the works Raphael saw, particularly those by da Vinci, changed and improved his style so much that it seemed "as if Raphael became another artist from his previous works."[1]

Art historian Heinrich Wölfflin claims Raphael became more "painterly" during his Florence years and developed increased realism in his work.[2] Da

16

Vinci's influence on Raphael is evident in his pyramid arrangement of figures within compositions and the way his subjects look directly at the viewer. Often, as with da Vinci's portrait of *Mona Lisa,* Raphael shows only three quarters of a subject's body.

The young artist's talent was soon recognized, and Raphael received requests from important patrons. Some of these commissions took him to Perugia, Siena, Venice, and back to Urbino, so it is not clear if Raphael was in Florence during Fra Girolamo Savonarola's reign of religious terror. Lorenzo de' Medici died in 1492, and his son, Piero, was driven from Florence two years later. Savonarola, a Catholic monk, took control of the city and proclaimed Jesus Christ to be Florence's only true ruler. Savonarola hated the Medicis and the humanism they fostered. Thousands of books, paintings, textiles, festival costumes, and jewelry were consumed in Savonarola's "bonfire of vanities" as he attempted to cleanse Florence of sin. Only works of art that "honored Christianity" were spared. Raphael's paintings and sketches likely escaped burning, since Savonarola considered works by Raphael's mentor, Pietro Perugino, morally acceptable.

Raphael painted the ideal beauty and sacred nature of the beliefs of his time and place, and his patrons' choices largely dictated his repetition of these religious themes. The favorite subject of the day was the madonna holding the infant Jesus. Anyone who could afford to pay was eager to have Raphael paint one. He eventually produced more than thirty, most of them during his years in Florence, although he continued this theme throughout his career. Though recognizable as being by Raphael, no two are the same. His later madonnas contain more figures, as the holy family becomes an extended family, with saints and patrons set against increasingly detailed backgrounds. Raphael's colors brightened with time, and more care was given to such details as the play of light upon clothing. Long treasured for their grace and the expression of that special bond between mother and child, Raphael's works are familiar from Christmas cards and postage stamps.

Madonna della Seggiola, or *Madonna of the Chair,* (1514) is an example of Michelangelo's influence on Raphael. Both mother and child look out at the viewer from a tondo, or round frame. The solid, massive figures, including John the Baptist, patron saint of Florence, occupy most of the space. The madonna's legs are pushed against the frame to make room for the baby on her lap. Her head is bound in the stylish scarf so popular in Renaissance Italy. Special attention has been given to detail and the effects of light upon the texture and color of garments.

"Today my wife and I went to the Pitti Palace," American author Nathaniel Hawthorne wrote in his diary on June 10, 1858. "The collection of pictures is the most interesting I have seen. . . . The most beautiful picture in the world, I am convinced, is Raphael's *Madonna della Seggiola*. I was familiar with it in a hundred engravings and copies, and therefore it shone upon one as with a familiar beauty, though infinitely more divine. . . . An artist was copying it, and producing certainly something very like a facsimile, yet leaving out that mysterious something that renders this picture a miracle."[3]

According to art historian James H. Beck, the most significant and complex painting from Raphael's Florence years was *The Entombment,* in which the artist leaves the style of Perugino behind. Here, Raphael "captures the character of his subjects."[4] Painted in 1507, it is known as the Baglioni Altarpiece, since it was commissioned by Atalanta Baglioni in memory of her son Grifonetto, who had been assassinated in 1500. This dramatic narrative painting, which shows people carrying the crucified Jesus to his tomb, is a long way from Raphael's gentle madonna-and-child portraits. The figure of Christ appears so lifeless that he may have been modeled from an actual corpse. To heighten the dramatic effect, the artist contrasts movements among the different figures. Raphael now shows more interest in expressing emotion through bodily movements and various facial expressions, such as the women reaching out to catch Jesus's mother as she faints. We do not observe figures simply weeping around the dead Christ as in other paintings of the period, but see men actually carrying Jesus's corpse to the tomb. One man even walks backward.

The Entombment also shows Michelangelo's influence upon Raphael. The artist studied the *David* statue and was familiar with Michelangelo's *Pietà*, which shows Mary holding the body of her crucified son.

Entombment (Baglioni Altarpiece). This altarpiece was stolen a century after Raphael ted it. The crosses of the crucifixion atop Calvary are silhouetted against the foreboding It was Raphael's first major commission after moving to Florence and shows his iarity with Michelangelo's sculpture.

Madonna del Baldacchino. This is the painting Raphael left unfinished when Pope Julius II summoned him to Rome. The saints arranged around the Madonna and Child and the flying angels holding the curtain open dramatize the painting. St. Peter and St. Bernard are on the left, with St. Augustine and St. James at right.

When Raphael was twenty-five, Pope Julius II invited him to take on the most important project of his life. Raphael was so excited by this job offer that he left for Rome without even finishing the painting he had been working on, *Madonna del Baldacchino,* or receiving pay from his patron.

Giorgio Vasari (1511–1574)

Much of what is known of Italian Renaissance artists comes from a best-seller written over 500 years ago. Vasari's *Lives of the Painters, Sculptors, and Architects* appeared in five volumes in 1550, with chapters on 120 artists from the early-fourteenth to the late-sixteenth century. A second edition was published in 1568. Dedicated to his patron Cosimo de' Medici, the Duke of Tuscany, Vasari's work remains an important source. He wrote, ". . . hoping that the example of so many able men and all the various details collected by my labours . . . will be of no little help to practicing artists as well as pleasing all those who follow and delight in the arts."[5]

Vasari means "makers of vases," and Giorgio Vasari's father was in fact a ceramic artist in Arezzo. Giorgio's first art teacher was his uncle, Luca Signorelli. During the revolt against the Medicis in 1527, a bench thrown out a window broke one arm of Michelangelo's *David.* Fragments lay in the piazza for three days until Vasari and a fellow student risked capture by soldiers to pick up the pieces.[6]

In 1529, Giorgio's father died of the plague, leaving Giorgio to support his mother and six siblings. He became a successful painter and architect, and also produced plays and created costumes for festivals. In 1563, Vasari founded Italy's first academy to train artists.[7]

Vasari designed the Uffizi in Florence as government offices. This series of horseshoe-shaped, arcaded buildings later became the first museum open to the public. Vasari also supervised the decoration of Palazzo Vecchio in Florence. In 1571, he was knighted by Pope Pius V.

Vasari collected drawings and was interested in artists' styles, and he loved gossip. Of all the biographies he wrote, the only artist he actually knew was Michelangelo, whose tomb he designed.

For Your Information

Uffizi in Florence, Italy

School of Athens (Stanza della Segnatura) is one of the most famous works in Western art and Raphael's most ambitious fresco. A lot of ancient Greek and Roman philosophy and history is happening here, yet Raphael manages to keep it all organized within his architectural space. Pope Julius II was determined to leave his mark on art and culture and knew genius when he saw it.

three

Raphael's Julian Period

It was Donato Bramante, Pope Julius's chief architect and art director, who recommended Raphael for his new job. In spite of their age difference, Raphael and Bramante had formed a lifelong friendship back in Urbino. Now the pope wanted frescoes for the walls of his private quarters inside the Vatican. Some artists were already at work, but when Julius II saw examples of Raphael's style, he dismissed them. The pope even ordered some paintings destroyed to clear the walls for Raphael.

Pope Julius's dream was to bring back the glory that had once been Imperial Rome. Artists and architects from all over Italy were moving there, yet Raphael felt he could compete with the best of them. As a child in his father's studio, he had learned how to manage a workshop and train apprentices. Raphael knew this new assignment would require assistants. With so many artists in Rome eager to learn painting at the side of a successful master, Raphael did not think it would be too difficult to set up his own studio.

Fresco means "fresh" in Italian. Careful planning is required for a fresco, because once the paint is on the wall, it is very difficult to make changes. The wall is first covered with a thin layer of plaster that is allowed to dry just enough to receive paint. Outlines of the planned work, called cartoons, are taped onto the wall in sections. Then these designs are poked with pins and brushed with charcoal. The images are applied to the damp plaster and bind to the wall as it dries. The artist puts down only what he plans to complete that day and must work fast—the wall dries quickly, particularly in warm weather. Frescoes were common in classical times, although

Greek and Roman artists used mats of woven reeds instead of paper car-
toons to transfer their designs.[1]

Stanza della Segnatura, which means "signature room," was originally
Pope Julius's personal library, but Vasari named it this because in his time it
was where popes signed documents.[2] The frescoes of these Raphael
Rooms, as they are also known, are still considered High Renaissance masterpieces. The major theme of the *Segnatura* is man's pursuit of knowledge.[3]
Completed in 1511, it is, according to Italian scholar Claudio Merlo, "the
greatest artistic celebration of humanism."[4]

On the ceiling, allegorical and historical figures symbolize theology, philosophy, poetry, and law: the four major divisions of knowledge according
to Renaissance thought. On one wall below, the *Disputa del Sacramento*
expresses the Renaissance belief that Christianity exists in harmony with
classical culture. Jesus appears above with the Madonna and St. John, surrounded by figures from the Old and New Testaments. Early church fathers,
along with important men from Raphael's own time, fill the lower section.

The School of Athens on the opposite wall honors human reason and
mankind's intellectual and scientific achievements. Great thinkers from the
past as well as from Raphael's day are shown teaching or deep in discus-
sion, thus forming a visual link between the ancient world and the
Renaissance. Each figure is individually painted and has his place in the harmony and balance of the whole design. Arches frame the central figures of
Greek philosophers Aristotle and Plato; Raphael painted a portrait of Leonardo da Vinci to represent Plato.

Raphael organized it all like a stage set, with the action taking place in
front of an architectural backdrop that serves to unify the whole scene. The
stooping figure on the right, holding a compass with which he makes a circle
on his tablet, is the Greek founder of geometry, Euclid (represented by a
portrait of Donato Bramante). At lower left, Pythagoras, the Greek mathematician who believed numbers to be the origin of all things, shows a
student the rules of musical proportions.[5]

Raphael included himself, wearing a black cap, among the figures standing on the right. Ptolemy, astrologer and astronomer of ancient Greece, his
back to the viewer, balances a globe in his left hand. Zoroaster is in front of

him, with his globe of the heavens. Diogenes, the founder of cynicism, who believed happiness came from indifference toward all earthly things, reclines on the steps. [6]

At the same time that Raphael was at work on *The School of Athens,* Michelangelo was behind locked doors, painting the ceiling of the Sistine Chapel. Bramante, as the pope's architect, had his own key to the chapel. Once, when Michelangelo was out of town, Bramante invited Raphael to sneak a peek at what Michelangelo had already completed. Raphael climbed up the scaffold and was amazed at the monumental figures with limbs that seemed to move as if alive.[7]

When Raphael returned to his own fresco, he removed several earlier images and repainted other figures. Most scholars believe the figure of Heraclitus seated on the steps, leaning on his elbow against a block of marble, was added later as a tribute to Michelangelo. In pose and bulk, Raphael's Heraclitus owes much to Jeremiah and other prophets on Michelangelo's Sistine ceiling.[8]

Ironically, Michelangelo did not appreciate this honor, especially when, urged by Bramante, Raphael generously offered to finish the other half of the Sistine ceiling. Competition among Renaissance artists was fierce, and Raphael and Michelangelo were both painting frescoes inside the Vatican at the same time and aiming to please the same patron. "When Michelangelo saw Raphael's work," Vasari wrote, "he was convinced, and rightly, that Bramante had deliberately done him that wrong for the sake of Raphael's profit and fame."[9]

A letter Michelangelo wrote more than twenty years after Raphael's death, on October 24, 1542, revealed his envy of the younger painter's success: "All the discord that was born between Pope Julius and me was from the envy of Bramante and of Raphael of Urbino . . . in order to ruin me. And Raphael had good reason for this, because everything he had in art, he had from me."[10]

Raphael and his assistants painted *The Liberation of St. Peter from Prison in the Stanza d'Eliodoro* to celebrate the expulsion of French forces from Italy and to reaffirm confidence in the papacy. Raphael cleverly incorporated the alcove and stone arches, which were parts of the original wall,

into his design. Peter, asleep in his cell, is awakened by an angel who leads him past the guards to freedom. The dramatic effect is heightened by the moonlight and glow of torches, reflected in the soldiers' armor. Art historians consider this fresco a landmark in art history because of this special treatment of light. Although the printing press was in use at this time and books available, most people still did not know how to read. Raphael and his assistants retold Bible stories and explained historical events by painting narrative frescoes in decorative detail.[11]

Raphael and his assistants had nearly completed the *Stanza d'Eliodoro* frescoes when Pope Julius II died on February 20, 1513, and Giovanni de' Medici was elected Pope Leo X. Only thirty-seven years old, and a son of Lorenzo de' Medici, he had been a cardinal since the age of thirteen. Like his predecessor, Leo was a great patron of the arts who collected Roman antiquities and longed to bring back the greatness of classical Rome. And, like Julius II, the new pope was a great admirer of Raphael's artistic abilities and courtly manners.

In 1514, Leo X commissioned Raphael to design loggias, or halls, as well as frescoes in a third Vatican room. *Stanza dell'Incendio di Borgo,* or the *Room of Fire in Borgo,* was intended to serve as Leo X's private dining room. Perugino had previously painted the ceiling there for Pope Julius II, and out of respect for his former teacher, Raphael insisted that it stay. The dramatic scene depicts a fire that broke out in St. Peter's Basilica (formerly called Borgo) in 847, and was put out by Pope Leo IV. The façade of old St. Peter's that was replaced by Bramante's new basilica can be seen here. According to art historian James H. Beck, Raphael "explored new and more complex spatial possibilities."[12]

Claudio Merlo, an Italian art historian, wrote that Raphael learned the blending of colors and the fusion of figures into space from da Vinci, while from Michelangelo, he learned to draw forms using the geometry of the spiral and the pyramid.[13]

Raphael's increasing interests in architecture and archaeology are evident in these Vatican frescoes. Raphael continually developed skills in new areas, and his wide range of subjects shows his willingness to experiment with different themes and techniques.

Donato Bramante (1444–1529)

Donato Bramante was born near Urbino and may have been related to Raphael. Trained as a painter, he worked for the Duke of Milan and the Sforza family in the 1480s, where he knew Leonardo da Vinci. After the French took control of Milan in 1499, Bramante moved to Rome.

Bramante was considered the greatest architect of his time, since his classical style marked the beginning of High Renaissance architecture. The central plan of his churches became the preferred form. San Pietro in Montorio was commissioned by Queen Isabella and King Ferdinand of Spain. They wanted a shrine built on the spot where St. Peter, founder of the Roman Catholic Church, was executed by Roman soldiers. Bramante designed the *Tempietto* ("little

Tempietto

temple"), as it came to be known, in 1502. It was completed in 1511. Considered one of the most important structures in the history of architecture, it marked a huge change from medieval churches and earlier Renaissance buildings. The harmony and balance of its domed, circular design was based on classical temples such as the Pantheon. Ancient Romans considered the circle the purest geometrical form, since it mirrored the order of the universe.

In 1506, Pope Julius II put Bramante in charge of papal architecture and art and assigned Bramante to rebuild St. Peter's Basilica. Raphael

assisted the older architect, then assumed supervision of the project after Bramante's death, calling it "a great weight on my shoulders."[14] Their designs were later superseded by others, including Michelangelo's.

Because Bramante used mathematical principles in architectural design, Raphael honored his old friend by depicting him as Euclid, the ancient Greek mathematician, in *The School of Athens*. In the central arch, Raphael revealed Bramante's St. Peter's design, its dome still uncapped.

Euclid detail from *The School of Athens*

Sistine Madonna. Raphael mastered the popular Renaissance Madonna theme during his Florence years. This work is designed like a stage set. Pope Sixtus died a martyr in Rome in 258 CE. and Saint Barbara, another Christian put to death for religious beliefs, kneels, gazing toward the cherubs.

four

"More Like a Prince Than a Painter"[1]

Raphael was always eager to advance his career. Though his life was relatively short, the volume and range of work he produced is truly amazing. He became the most successful painter in Rome, a city full of gifted artists. The portraits he painted, his popular madonnas, and the *Stanza della Segnatura* earned him a reputation for excellence as well as punctuality. Raphael's studio was the busiest in Rome, for he was the first choice of most merchants, bankers, and princes who wanted their portraits painted or likenesses made for persons they wished to marry. Raphael was the man about town, invited to dine with people of the highest social rank or to join their hunting parties and other pleasurable outings.

" 'You go about with a retinue like a prince,' " Michelangelo told Raphael, according to Vasari. " 'And you, Michelangelo, go about alone,' replied Raphael, 'like a hangman.' . . . There came to Raffaelo a great increase of glory, and likewise of rewards; and for this reason, in order to leave some memorial of himself, he caused a place to be built in the Borgo Nuovo at Rome, with columns made of cast stucco under Bramante's direction."[2]

Raphael summed up the rewards of fame, as well as his thoughts on marriage, in a letter to Simone Ciarla, his uncle in Urbino, dated July 1, 1514: ". . . as regards taking a bride, I reply that I am extremely happy, and thank God continuously that I didn't accept her—the one you first wanted me to have—or the other one. And in this I was wiser than you, who wanted to give her to me. I am certain that now, even you understand that I would not be in the place where I am if I had done as you wished. For as of today, I find myself to be worth in Rome 3000 gold ducats and a yearly income of 50 gold scudi that His Holiness has given me for work at St. Peter's, and 300 gold ducats for expenses, which I will receive as long as I live; and I am certain to have more. Then I am paid for whatever work I decide to do on my own; and I have begun to paint another room for His Holiness, which will amount to 1,200 gold ducats. . . . I purposely allowed myself to digress from the topic of taking a wife. But to return to the subject, I reply that Cardinal Bibbiena wants to give me a relative of his in marriage. With your permission, and that of my uncle the priest, I promised."[3]

Raphael never married. The cardinal's niece died before the wedding. After Raphael's death, her remains were placed in his tomb. Vasari wrote that Raphael kept postponing marriage because it was hinted that he "might be rewarded with the red hat" for his labors at the Vatican and excellent service to popes. This meant Raphael expected to be appointed a cardinal, and cardinals could not be married.[4]

Raphael continually worked to improve his range of artistic skills, always eager to learn new techniques. According to art historian James H. Beck, Raphael's drawing demonstrates his mastery of the line. His controlled draftsmanship was "never entirely subordinated to painterly qualities."[5]

The artist's drawings survive in museums and private collections, so one can study his creative processes and see how he experimented with the placement of figures within his compositions. One of Raphael's madonnas turns so that she looks out of the picture. He makes several saints kneel, and in another sketch shows them standing or gesturing—yet he always strives for balance in the whole composition. Raphael sketched details for his architectural settings and landscape backgrounds. He experimented with various movements of arms and legs and the twist of the torso. He draws heads and hands in different poses, practicing to get them right, for Raphael was ever the perfectionist. He solves the visual challenge of how drapery looks as it falls across a body. He analyzes the way light is reflected on a velvet cape or silk veil. Raphael used many of his drawings for teaching, just as his father and Perugino had. Raphael is still considered

Studies for the Transfiguration. Raphael made hundreds of preliminary drawings for his finished paintings. He sketched live models in different poses, experimenting with placement of heads and hands, and trying out various facial expressions.

an outstanding master of color as well as one of the greatest draftsmen of all time.

Raphael eventually directed one of the largest studios ever assembled under one master. Vasari claimed that fifty painters followed Raphael to the Vatican daily. He was an excellent manager and teacher, requiring his students to work diligently at improving their skills. Raphael generously helped other artists, even leaving his own work to do so, "treating them as sons, rather than mechanics."[6] They modeled for the master and painted one another. Even the youngest apprentices could prepare walls for frescoes, help build scaffolding, or paint the sky on a wood panel. They worked alongside their master, so Raphael knew the special abilities of every student.[7]

The master and his assistants painted the ceilings and walls of Pope Leo's loggia of thirteen bays, each illustrating a different Bible story. This became known as Raphael's Bible.

The *Sistine Madonna* is probably Raphael's most famous painting. Nothing is left to chance in this carefully planned composition. Commissioned to hang high above the altar of San Sisto Church in Piacenza, the viewer looks up at the standing madonna, floating on a bank of clouds with *putti*, or cherubs. The painting is like a window, curtains opened to show viewers the special event, attended by Saint Barbara and Pope Sixtus II. The *putti* leaning against the bottom of the frame may seem familiar—they were reproduced as Christmas stamps. One cherub lacks a wing. This was no mistake on Raphael's part, but a conscious choice, since he thought a second wing might distract the viewer from focusing on the madonna and child. The model for the *Sistine Madonna* was Raphael's longtime mistress, Margherita Luti from Siena, known as *La Fornarina* or "the baker's daughter." Her lovely face appears in many of Raphael's paintings.

According to art historians Roger Jones and Nicholas Penny, "From early in his career, Raphael showed special skill at portraiture which was strongly influenced by Leonardo da Vinci, especially in his arrangement of figures. Raphael's early portraits often have folded arms in the same position as *Mona Lisa*'s, with a three-fourths turn of the body and half-length

Pope Leo X with Two Cardinals. Considered one of the best group portraits ever painted, the irony is that the two cardinals (cousins of the pope) were added later. Scholars think the artist's careful attention to detail indicates familiarly with Flemish art, which, indeed, Raphael saw as a boy in the ducal palace at Urbino.

seated pose which provides the base for a balanced, pyramidal composition."[8]

Raphael carefully considered the personality of his sitters before painting their portraits, since each one depicts an individual character. "While we may term other works paintings, those of Raphael are living things," Vasari wrote. "The flesh palpitates; the breath comes and goes, every organ lives, life pulsates everywhere."[9]

Pope Leo X with Two Cardinals (1517–1518) was painted for a Medici wedding gift, and is considered one of the finest group portraits ever painted. Vasari commented: ". . . all these things executed with such confidence and control that one may believe no master is able or is ever likely to do better."[10] X-ray examination revealed that the cardinals' portraits were added afterward, perhaps by Raphael's star pupil, Giulio Romano. Like Leo X, these cardinals were Medici cousins and thus were trusted by the pope (it was painted not long after an attempt on Leo's life by members of the College of Cardinals).[11] Raphael, the master of detail, captured the velvet texture of Pope Leo's vestments lined with white fur; the glint of gold and shimmer of silk; even the reflection of light upon the brass knob of the chair and the silver bell, magnifying glass, and the illuminated manuscript lying on the table. As Raphael's responsibilities increased, he assigned more work to his growing number of assistants, although he continued to sketch all designs and supervise each commission.

Following Bramante's death, Pope Leo X appointed Raphael as Chief Architect of St. Peter's Basilica. "The Holy Father, in honoring me, has laid a heavy burden upon my shoulders; the charge of the building of St. Peter's," Raphael wrote Baldassare Castiglione in 1514. "I hope I shall not sink under it; the model I have made for it pleases His Holiness and has been praised by many persons of taste. But my thoughts rise still higher. I should like to revive the handsome forms of the buildings of the ancients."[12]

This letter shows Raphael's growing interest in architecture and archaeology, each of which would become a major focus for the artist for the rest of his life.

Baldassare Castiglione (1478–1529)

Raphael and Castiglione first met in Urbino and remained close friends. Baldassare spent his early years in the Court of Milan, then served the Montefeltro family from 1504 to 1516. The Duke of Urbino even sent him as an emissary to England to retrieve the Order of the Garter awarded the duke by Henry VII.

Castiglione wrote *The Book of the Courtier* describing life at the court of Urbino when Guidobaldo, son of Federico da Montefeltro, ruled and the hill town was a cultural center. The book contains politics and philosophy and even includes instructions for playing games. Ideas are presented through dialogue expressed by members of the court and led by Elisabetta Gonzaga, Duchess of Urbino. The book went through many printings and translations and served as the model for court behavior throughout Europe. It remains a source for understanding Renaissance life. The "universal man" was Castiglione's ideal and he paid tribute to Raphael as "talented and charming . . . the model of a courtier and artist."[13]

As a career diplomat and ambassador to Rome, Castiglione was frequently away from home. He wanted Raphael to paint his portrait so that his family would remember him. This High Renaissance gentleman showed qualities of wisdom, dignity, and humanity. The pyramid composition with hands clasped makes one think of da Vinci's *Mona Lisa*. Dressed in somber colors, Castiglione looks directly out at the viewer, his face framed by his high collar and stylish hat. His intelligence is emphasized by his white scarf and gold button.

"Only your portrait, painted by Raphael's hand bringing back your features, comes near to relieving my sorrows," Castiglione's wife wrote. "I make tender approaches to it, I smile, I joke or speak, just as if it could answer. . . . Your son recognizes his father, and greets him with childish talk."[14]

Portrait of Baldassare Castiglione, 1515. As a portrait painter, Raphael was interested in revealing the personality of his sitters. Count Castiglione was a good friend of the artist and his picture is considered a brilliant character study. Castiglione's *Book of the Courtier* brought him fame throughout Europe as the ideal Renaissance man.

The Transfiguration, Raphael's last major work, shows how his style changed in the final years of his short life. Art historians don't know how much of this was painted by Raphael and how much by his assistants, though all agree the overall design was by the master.

Raphael Seeks "Rome in Rome"

Following Bramante's death in 1514, Pope Leo X appointed Raphael chief architect in charge of all buildings and paintings for the Vatican. The artist always welcomed a new challenge, so he was delighted when Pope Leo "decided he would have some very rich tapestries made in gold and silk" to cover the walls of the Sistine Chapel below Michelangelo's ceiling. The pontiff commissioned Raphael to create ten designs depicting events in the lives of St. Peter and St. Paul. Raphael and his assistants had to draw the cartoons in reverse so that weavers could reproduce them on their looms in Brussels. Vasari thought these tapestries were "created by a miracle rather than by human skill."[1] Pope Leo X's pursuit of culture and art eventually bankrupted the papacy. After his death, Raphael's tapestries had to be pawned to pay for the installation of the next pope.

Raphael began designing Villa Madama for the pope's family in 1517. This was to be a private retreat for Cardinal Giulio de' Medici (who would later become Pope Clement VII). Although unfinished at the time of Raphael's death, this was an important example of the Renaissance ideal of combining architecture, sculpture, painting, landscape, and decoration in one work. The architectural treasure with columns and circular courtyard surrounded by gardens had its source in ancient Roman villas. Architectural details were inspired by classical decoration on temple friezes and Roman sarcophagi.

The ruins of ancient Rome were all around Raphael. Almost daily, construction crews digging foundations for new buildings or farmers planting fields would uncover a broken column, friezes, or sculptures from another classical temple or villa. Both of Raphael's patron popes boasted collections of archaeological discoveries. Raphael lamented the destruction of Rome by the Goths, and in his own time by construction crews using classical ruins for building materials. "Since I have been in Rome which is not yet 12 years, many beautiful things have been ruined," Raphael wrote. He said he "had been very diligent in studying antiquities and used much care in finding and measuring them. . . . Having devoted much study to these antiquities and taken no little trouble to seek them out in detail and measure them with care, constantly reading the good authors and comparing their descriptions with the monuments, I think I have acquired some knowledge of ancient architecture. To know about such an excellent subject gives me the greatest pleasure, but at the same time it is very painful to see how miserably lacerated is this noble and beautiful city."[2]

In August 1515, Pope Leo X appointed Raphael superintendent of Roman antiquities. As city planner, it was his job to oversee the preservation of ancient monuments. The pontiff decreed no workers be allowed to use any stones with inscriptions or carvings for building, without Raphael's permission. For at least a century following Raphael's death, his sketches of ancient Roman sites and sculptures were part of every academic education.[3]

Raphael was re-creating a map of ancient Rome for each section of the city, intending to show exactly which ancient buildings stood where. Drawing upon his rich knowledge of archaeology, Raphael planned to locate the old Roman monuments on grids. He continually researched new discoveries in the classical texts. Unfortunately, he was able to complete only one of Rome's fourteen sections before his death.

Celio Calcagnini, a friend and admirer of the artist, wrote of Raphael's archaeological accomplishments, "So many heroes and such a long time it took to build Rome! So many enemies and so many centuries it took to destroy it! Now Raphael is seeking Rome in Rome and finding it. To seek is the sign of a great man; to find—of a god."[4]

Raphael died on his thirty-seventh birthday—April 6, 1520—at the peak of his career. A hard worker all his life, he had given his best to an increasing number of projects and patrons. Yet Raphael also enjoyed the pleasures of life. According to Vasari, after one all-night party, the artist returned home with a mysterious fever. He lay ill fifteen days, during which time doctors bled him, according to medical treatment of that time, "until he grew faint." Raphael dictated his last will and testament, in which he provided for his beloved mistress Margherita, and bequeathed his studio with all its art materials to his assistants. At the time of his death, Raphael's fortune was estimated to be 16,000 ducats.

Count Baldassare Castiglione mourned his good friend, especially regretting the archaeological projects that Raphael would never finish.

With the genius of your art, Raffaello,
You likewise healed Rome's mutilated city:
It was an empty Husk, destroyed through sword and
Fire, and decayed through age.
You, nonetheless, restored its life
And revived its ancient beauty.
Your act aroused the envy of the jealous gods;
Their penalty was your death—untimely and undeserved.
What time eroded, you dared revive,
And thus, defied the law of mortal death.
Your sad demise while in the bloom of youth
Stands as grim warning to us all of death's dark doom.[5]

The Transfiguration was the artist's last major work. Commissioned by Cardinal Giulio de' Medici, the future Pope Clement VII, for the cathedral in Narbonne, France, it was not quite finished at the time of his death. The huge altarpiece finally made it to France in 1797, but as Napoleonic loot. It was returned to the Vatican in 1815. A cleaning 450 years after it was painted revealed the brilliant colors and extraordinary lighting Raphael used to dramatize the scene of a boy supposedly possessed by the devil. Theatrical gestures and experimental lighting in the upper and lower halves of the painting emphasized the contrast between man's earthly troubles and the peacefulness of the spiritual realm.

The Transfiguration was placed by Raphael's head as his body lay in state. According to Vasari, "the sight of that living picture in contrast with the dead body caused the hearts of all who beheld it to burst with sorrow." Raphael was "highly praised and publicly mourned."[6] In the procession from the artist's studio to the Pantheon, one eyewitness reported that the artist's coffin was accompanied by one hundred painters, all bearing torches.

In his will, Raphael expressed his wish to be buried in the Pantheon, one of his favorite classical buildings, and left 1,500 ducats for its interior restoration. He requested that his tomb be placed beneath an altar and below a statue of the Virgin Mary. This symbolized the merging of classical and Christian cultures, both revered by the artist. Lorenzo Lotti, one of Raphael's assistants, modeled the Virgin after an ancient Roman statue of Venus that the artist had admired.

Pietro Bembo (1470–1547), a Venetian writer associated with the Court of Urbino who later became a cardinal, wrote the following for his friend's tomb: *Here lies that famous Raphael by whom Nature feared to be outdone while he lived and when he died, feared Herself would die.*

Bembo also penned this epitaph:

Raffaello Santi, the son of Giovanni of Urbino
Eminent painter, Rival of the Ancients.
Looking upon his lifelike images
You can thus behold the unification of nature and art.
Through his paintings and architecture
He increased the glory of Popes Julius II and Leo X
He lived for 37 years in complete perfection
And died on the day of his birth[7]

"When this noble craftsman died," wrote Vasari, "the art of painting might well have died with him; for when Raphael closed his eyes, painting was left as if blind."[8]

Lady with a Veil (La Donna Velata). Most art historians believe this to be another portrait of Margherita Luti (*La Fornarina* or the Baker's Daughter) the love of Raphael's life and his favorite model. The artist's mastery of color and ability to paint textures continually improved. Vasari said this was "a most beautiful portrait which seems alive."[9]

For centuries, Raphael was regarded as the perfect painter, the yardstick by which all other artists were measured. He was the model whom other painters were told to copy in order to learn how to paint correctly.[10]

Raphael's works became sources for other artists and inspirations for generations of painters. The French National Academy focused chiefly on Raphael. French painter Nicolas Poussin (1594–1665) traveled to Italy to view Raphael's works and ended up spending most of his life there. Neoclassicists Jacques-Louis David (1748–1825) and Jean-Auguste Ingres (1780–1867), who set the standard for French nineteenth-century art, lived in Italy for a time, hoping to absorb Raphael. Ingres considered the Renaissance master "the essence of classicism,"[11] rejecting modern art for the past in his own paintings. Today, Raphael remains one of the most familiar and universally admired of all artists.

The Patronage of Chigi

Raphael was fortunate in his patrons. Not only was he favored by two popes, he was the choice of the richest man in Italy, Agostino Chigi. A merchant and banker originally from Siena, Chigi was also in charge of all financial affairs for Pope Julius II.

Raphael's *Triumph of Galatea*

In 1512, Chigi commissioned Raphael to decorate the loggia of his new palace, Villa Farnesina, located outside Rome. The banker was particularly fond of the classics and wanted frescoes depicting earth and sea gods from Greek and Roman mythology. Although the series was never completed, *The Triumph of Galatea* was the first purely mythological theme Raphael ever painted.

Polyphemus pursues the goddess Galatea, who attempts escape by riding the waves on a shell pulled by dolphins, the wind blowing her hair and cloak. Cherubs overhead shoot arrows at Galatea, while sea nymphs are carried off by tritons blowing their horns. The viewer's attention is focused on Galatea, whose body, draped in red, twists and turns dramatically. The upraised arms of several sea gods frame the goddess. *The Triumph of Galatea* shows the influence of Roman sarcophagi designs on Raphael's work.

Galatea supposedly represented female perfection. In a letter to Baldassare Castiglione, Raphael wrote: "To paint a beautiful woman I would need to look upon many and take the best from each. As there is a shortage of both good judges and of beautiful women, I make use of a certain idea that comes from my mind."[12]

In 1513, Chigi commissioned Raphael to decorate family chapels at Santa Maria della Pace and Santa Maria del Popolo. These chapel designs set a new standard in which painting, sculpture, architecture, stucco, and mosaic were integrated, something Raphael greatly admired in studying the ruins of the Roman emperor Nero's Golden House.

1483	Raffaello Sanzio is born on April 6 in Urbino, in central Italy, to Magia di Battista Ciarla and court painter and poet Giovanni Santi.
1491	Raphael's mother dies on October 7.
1494	Raphael's father dies on August 1. His uncle, Simone Ciarla, becomes his guardian. He inherits his father's workshop
1495–1499	He probably serves apprenticeship under Pietro Vanucci or *Perugino* in Perugia.
1499	Raphael receives his first known commission, for an altarpiece in Città di Castello.
1500	Raphael may have worked as an assistant to Perugino.
1501–1508	Raphael paints commissions in Urbino, Perugia, Siena, and Florence.
1504	Raphael paints *Marriage of the Virgin* (considered the end of his Perugino phase). He moves to Florence, where he studies works of Leonardo da Vinci and Michelangelo; Michelangelo's *David* is installed.
1505–1507	Raphael receives a commission for an altarpiece and fresco in Perugia; paints *Madonna of the Meadow* and other madonnas, as well as portraits. Atalanta Baglioni hires Raphael to paint altarpiece *The Entombment* (signed and dated 1507). He paints *Madonna of the Goldfinch* or *Madonna del Cardellino* before moving to Rome.
1508	He moves to Rome and begins *Stanza della Segnatura* frescoes in the pope's private apartments in the Vatican.
1509	Raphael is appointed *scriptor brevium,* or papal scribe, on October 4.
1511	Agostino Chigi becomes a patron of Raphael, who paints his only major mythological work, *The Triumph of Galatea,* for the wealthy banker. Raphael completes *The School of Athens* and paints *Portrait of Pope Julius II* (who vowed not to shave off his beard until Italy was free from French occupation).
1512–1513	Raphael continues working at Villa Farnesina under Chigi's patronage and begins Santa Maria del Popolo.
1513	Pope Julius II dies on February 20. Giovanni de' Medici is elected Pope Leo X. Raphael paints *Madonna of the Chair* and *Sistine Madonna.*
1514	Bramante dies on March 11, and Raphael is appointed to succeed him as papal architect in charge of overseeing design and construction of St. Peter's Basilica.
1515	Pope Leo X appoints Raphael superintendent of Roman antiquities; he begins work on *Map of Ancient Rome.*
1516–1519	Raphael designs cartoons for a series of tapestries in the Sistine Chapel.
1517–1518	Raphael designs Villa Madama, integrating architecture, painting, landscape, and decorative arts; paints a portrait of *Pope Leo X* and begins *The Transfiguration.*
1519	In December, his completed tapestries are exhibited in the Sistine Chapel. Raphael continues working on his *Map of Ancient Rome.*
1520	Raphael dies on his birthday and is buried in the Pantheon, according to his wishes. Agostino Chigi dies.
1523	Perugino dies.

SELECTED WORKS

CHAPTER NOTES

Chapter 1 The Court Painter's Son
1. Irwin Shapiro, *The Golden Book of the Renaissance* (New York: Golden Press, 1962), p. 144.
2. Bette Talvacchia, *Raphael* (New York: Phaidon Press, 2007), p. 25.
3. Hugo Chapman, Tom Henry, and Carol Plazzotta, *Raphael: From Urbino to Rome* (London: National Gallery, 2004), p. 140.
4. James H. Beck, *Raphael* (New York: Harry N. Abrams, 1976), p. 90.
5. Vasari, Giorgio. "Life of Raphael of Urbino, Painter and Architect, 1483–1520," *Lives of the Painters, Sculptors, and Architects* (Italy, 1550; Second Edition, 1568).
6. Roger Jones and Nicholas Penny, *Raphael* (New Haven, CT: Yale University Press, 1987), p. 5.
7. Shapiro, pp. 143–144.

8. Bruce Cole, *The Renaissance Artist at Work: From Pisano to Titian* (New York: Harper and Row, 1983), p. 3.
9. Claudio Merlo, *Three Masters of the Renaissance: Leonardo, Michelangelo, Raphael* (Hauppauge, New York: Barron's, 1999), p. 51.

Chapter 2 Florence: "School of the World"
1. Giorgio Vasari, *Artists of the Renaissance: A Selection from Lives of the Artists,* translated by George Bull (New York: Viking, 1978), p. 212.
2. Heinrich Wölfflin, *Classic Art: An Introduction to the Italian Renaissance* (New York: Phaidon Press, 1952), p. 73.
3. Nicoletta Baldini, *Raphael,* preface by Michele Prisco (New York: Rizzoli, 2005), p. 7.
4. James H. Beck, *Raphael* (New York: Harry N. Abrams, 1976), p. 16.
5. Vasari, p. 11.

6. Giorgio Vasari, *The Great Masters: Giotto, Botticelli, Leonardo, Raphael, Michelangelo & Titian,* translated by Gaston du C. de Vere (London: Beaux Arts Editions, 1986), pp. 9–10.

7. Ibid., p. 8.

Chapter 3 Raphael's Julian Period

1. Bruce Cole, *The Renaissance Artist at Work: From Pisano to Titian* (New York: Harper and Row, 1983), p. 78.

2. James H. Beck, *Raphael* (New York: Harry N. Abrams, 1976), p. 28.

3. Nicoletta Baldini, *Raphael,* preface by Michele Prisco (New York: Rizzoli, 2005), p. 116.

4. Claudio Merlo, *Three Masters of the Renaissance: Leonardo, Michelangelo, Raphael* (Hauppauge, New York: Barron's, 1999), p. 100.

5. Ibid., p. 102.

6. Ibid., p. 103.

7. Rona Goffen, *Renaissance Rivals: Michelangelo, Leonardo, Raphael, Titian* (New Haven, CT: Yale University Press, 2002), p. vi.

8. Ibid., p. 121.

9. Giorgio Vasari, *Artists of the Renaissance: A Selection from Lives of the Artists,* translated by George Bull (New York: Viking, 1978), p. 218.

10. Goffen, p. 171.

11. Vasari, p. 219.

12. Beck, pp. 37, 154.

13. Merlo, p. 65.

14. Roger Jones and Nicholas Penny, *Raphael* (New Haven, CT: Yale University Press, 1987), p. 215.

Chapter 4 "More Like a Prince Than a Painter"

1. Giorgio Vasari, *Artists of the Renaissance: A Selection from Lives of the Artists,* translated by George Bull (New York: Viking, 1978), p. 231.

2. Ibid., p. 225.

3. Bette Talvacchia, *Raphael* (New York: Phaidon Press, 2007), p. 106.

4. Ibid., p. 112.

5. James H. Beck, *Raphael* (New York: Harry N. Abrams, 1976), p. 150.

6. Roger Jones and Nicholas Penny, *Raphael* (New Haven, CT: Yale University Press, 1987), p. 197.

7. Bruce Cole, *The Renaissance Artist at Work: From Pisano to Titian* (New York: Harper and Row, 1983), p. 15.

8. Jones and Penny, p. 29.

9. Vasari, p. 208.

10. Giorgio Vasari, *The Great Masters: Giotto, Botticelli, Leonardo, Raphael, Michelangelo & Titian,* translated by Gaston du C. de Vere (London: Beaux Arts Editions, 1986), pp. 168–169.

11. Beck, p. 47.

12. Jones and Penny, p. 215.

13. Baldassare Castiglione, *The Book of the Courtier* (Italy, 1528), n.p.

14. David Alan Brown and Jane Van Nimmen, *Raphael and the Beautiful Banker: The Story of the Bindo Altoviti Portrait* (New Haven, CT: Yale University Press, 2005), p. 25.

Chapter 5 Raphael Seeks "Rome in Rome"

1. Giorgio Vasari, *Artists of the Renaissance: A Selection from Lives of the Artists,* translated by George Bull (New York: Viking, 1978), pp. 227–228.

2. Roger Jones and Nicholas Penny, *Raphael* (New Haven, CT: Yale University Press, 1987), p. 199.

3. Ibid.

4. Vasari, p. 231.

5. Nicoletta Baldini, *Raphael,* preface by Michele Prisco (New York: Rizzoli, 2005), pp. 66–67.

6. Rona Goffen, *Renaissance Rivals: Michelangelo, Leonardo, Raphael, Titian* (New Haven, CT: Yale University Press, 2002), p. 254.

7. Giorgio Vasari, *The Great Masters: Giotto, Botticelli, Leonardo, Raphael, Michelangelo & Titian,* translated by Gaston du C. de Vere (London: Beaux Arts Editions, 1986), p. 203.

8. Giorgio Vasari, *Artists of the Renaissance,* p. 231.

9. Hugo Chapman, Tom Henry, and Carol Plazzota. *Raphael: From Urbino to Rome* (London: Yale University Press) 2004, p. 278.

10. Marcia Hall, editor, *Raphael's "School of Athens"* (London: Cambridge University Press, 1997), p. 26.

11. "Raphael," *Encyclopedia of World Art* (New York: McGraw Hill Book Co., 1972), p. 865.

12. Jones and Penny, p. 215.

FURTHER READING

For Young Adults

Klein, Adam G. *Raphael.* Checkerboard Biography Library, Great Artists. Edina, MN: ABDO Publishing Company, 2006.

Muhlberger, Richard. *What Makes a Raphael a Raphael?* New York: Viking, 1993.

Venezia, Mike. *Raphael.* New York: Grolier, 2001.

Zuffi, Stefano. *Renaissance Painting: The Golden Age of European Art.* Hauppauge, NY: Barron's, 2000.

Works Consulted

Baldini, Nicoletta. *Raphael.* Preface by Michele Prisco. New York: Rizzoli, 2005.

Beck, James H. *Raphael.* New York: Harry N. Abrams, 1976.

———. *Raphael: The Stanza della Segnatura, Rome.* New York: George Braziller, 1993.

Brown, David Alan, and Jane Van Nimmen. *Raphael and the Beautiful Banker: The Story of the Bindo Altoviti Portrait.* New Haven, CT: Yale University Press, 2005.

Castiglione, Baldassare. *The Book of the Courtier.* Italy, 1528.

Chapman, Hugo, Tom Henry, and Carol Plazzotta. *Raphael: From Urbino to Rome.* London: National Gallery, 2004.

Cole, Alison. *Virtue & Magnificence: Art of the Italian Renaissance Courts.* New York: Harry N. Abrams, 1995.

Cole, Bruce. *The Renaissance Artist at Work: From Pisano to Titian.* New York: Harper and Row, 1983.

Freedberg, S. J. *Painting of the High Renaissance in Rome & Florence.* Cambridge, MA: Harvard University Press, 1961.

Goffen, Rona. *Renaissance Rivals: Michelangelo, Leonardo, Raphael, Titian.* New Haven, CT: Yale University Press, 2002.

Hall, Marcia, editor. *Raphael's "School of Athens."* London: Cambridge University Press, 1997.

Jones, Roger, and Nicholas Penny. *Raphael.* New Haven, CT: Yale University Press, 1987.

Lewis, Richard, and Susan I. Lewis. *The Power of Art.* New York: Harcourt Brace College Publishers, 1994.

Merlo, Claudio. *Three Masters of the Renaissance: Leonardo, Michelangelo,*

Raphael. Hauppauge, New York: Barron's, 1999.

Nasso, Claudio, and Tim Stroud. *Raphael: Grace and Beauty.* Milan, Italy: Skira, 2001.

Santi, Raphael. "Letter to Count Castiglione, Rome, 1514." Bellori. *Discorso sull'idea, Introduction to Lives, 1664,* "Raphael," *Encyclopedia of World Art,* New York: McGraw-Hill, 1972.

Shapiro, Irwin. *The Golden Book of the Renaissance.* New York: Golden Press, 1962.

Talvacchia, Bette. *Raphael.* New York: Phaidon Press, 2007.

Thoenes, Christof. *Raphael: 1483–1520.* Translated by Karen Williams. Koln, Germany: Taschen, 2005.

Vasari, Giorgio. *Artists of the Renaissance: A Selection from Lives of the Artists.* "Life of Raphael of Urbino: Painter & Architect, 1483–1520." Italy: 1550; 1568 (facsimile edition). Translated by George Bull. New York: Viking Press, 1978, pp. 207–231.

Vasari, Giorgio. *The Great Masters: Giotto, Botticelli, Leonardo, Raphael, Michelangelo & Titian.* Translated by Gaston du C. de Vere. London & Chicago: Beaux Arts Editions, 1986.

Ventura, Piero. *Great Painters.* New York: G. P. Putnam's Sons, 1984.

Wölfflin, Heinrich. *Classic Art: An Introduction to the Italian Renaissance.* New York: Phaidon Press, 1952.

Wright, Susan. *The Renaissance: Masterpieces of Art and Architecture.* New York: Smithmark Publishers, 1997.

On the Internet

The Artchive: Raphael (Raffaello Sanzio)
    www.artchive.com/artchive/R/raphael.html

Catholic Encyclopedia: Raphael
    http://www.newadvent.org/cathen/12640c.htm

Virtual Tour of Vatican:
    http://mv.vatican.va/3_EN/pages/MV_Visite.html

Web Gallery of Art: Raffaello Sanzio
    http://www.wga.hu/frames-e.html?/bio/r/raphael/biograph.html

WebMuseum, Paris: Raphael
    http://www.ibiblio.org/wm/paint/auth/raphael

GLOSSARY

allegory (AL-ih-gor-ee)—A literary or pictorial work in which the subjects represent symbols that illustrate religious ideas or moral principles.

altarpiece (AHL-tur-pees)—A painting or panel located above the altar in a church or chapel and usually illustrated with religious figures and Christian themes.

cartoon (kar-TOON)—A sketch the same size as a planned fresco that is transferred onto the wall by punching holes along the lines, then dabbing these holes with charcoal powder to outline the painting.

chiaroscuro (kee-AIR-oh-SKYUR-oh)—The technique of using light and shadow to create a three-dimensional illusion. Leonardo da Vinci called it the "soul of painting."

classical (KLAA-sih-kul)—Pertaining to the art, literature, and/or culture of ancient Greece and Rome.

commission (kuh-MIH-shun)—To employ an artist, sculptor, or architect to create a specific work, usually one of the patron's choice.

condottiere (kon-duh-TYAIR-ee)—The captain or leader of mercenary soldiers, serving under a *condotta* or contract to fight for a particular city-state or prince.

contrapasto (kon-trah-PAHS-toh)—The swing of the body or swiveling motion seen in classical sculpture and adapted by Leonardo da Vinci, Michelangelo, and Raphael in many of their own works. With the head turned away from the torso in a three-quarter view, figures seem more realistic.

courtier (KOR-tee-ur)—The member of a royal court who may be a relative of the ruler, an appointed official, or someone in service to a duke or king.

ducal (DOO-kul)—Pertaining to a duke or dukedom.

humanism (HYOO-muh-nih-zim)—The philosophy focused on human ideas and man's mental and physical abilities and achievements, rather than religion; the cultural and intellectual movement during the Renaissance that emphasized the secular world as a result of the influence of classical Greek and Roman civilization.

loggia (LOH-jee-uh)—An open gallery or arcade with a roof running along the front or side of a building.

perspective (pur-SPEK-tiv)—The method of showing distance in three-dimensional depth on a two-dimensional surface, using special painting techniques.

pontiff (PON-tif)—Another name for the elected head of the Roman Catholic Church, who is based in the Vatican in Rome; papal /papacy also pertain to the pope, who is also known as the Holy Father.

sanguine (SAAN-gwin)—A red pencil that is made from rust-colored clay and used for drawing.

sarcophagus (sar-KAH-fuh-gus)—Ancient Roman stone coffins, usually decorated with carved figures and action scenes known as friezes. Hundreds of broken sarcophagi (sar-KAH-fuh-guy) were found among classical ruins in Rome and all over Italy and had a great influence on Raphael and other Renaissance artists.

stanza (STAN-zuh)—The Italian word for room or hall; the plural form is *stanze* (STAN-zay).

sfumato (sfoo-MAH-toh)—Blurry or vanished, from the Italian word *fumo* (smoke); a manner of painting that gives the subject a softened effect (particularly evident in *Mona Lisa* and other works by Leonardo da Vinci); the technique of allowing tones and colors to shade or dissolve into one another so that light seems to radiate from inside the subject.

tondo—A circular painting.

INDEX